This book is dedicated
to all children who,
like Camila and Samantha, want
to be artists and to all adults who,
like Carmen Campoy and
Mary Anderson, love art.

May you all explore
your own creativity.

A picture

is a work of art
created by the painter.

You

are a work of art
created by life.

BLUE and GREEN

Alma Flor Ada
F. Isabel Campoy

ALFAGUARA
YOUNG READERS
SANTILLANA

Originally published in Spanish as Azul y verde

Art Director: Felipe Dávalos
Design: Arroyo + Cerda S.C.
Editor: Norman Duarte

Cover: Diego Velázquez, Las Meninas

Santillana USA Publishing Company, Inc.
2023 NW 84th Avenue
Miami, FL 33122

The authors gratefully acknowledge the editorial assistance
of Debra Luna.

Art A: Blue and Green

ISBN: 1-58105-574-9

Published in the United States
Printen in Colombia by D'vinni S.A.
14 13 12 11 10   3 4 5 6 7 8 9 10

Las Meninas
Diego Velázquez

On Sundays,
Sundays in the spring,
I like to go for a walk,
dressed in pink, all pink.

Dolores Asúnsolo at Age Eleven
Alfredo Ramos

 One girl, dressed in pink.

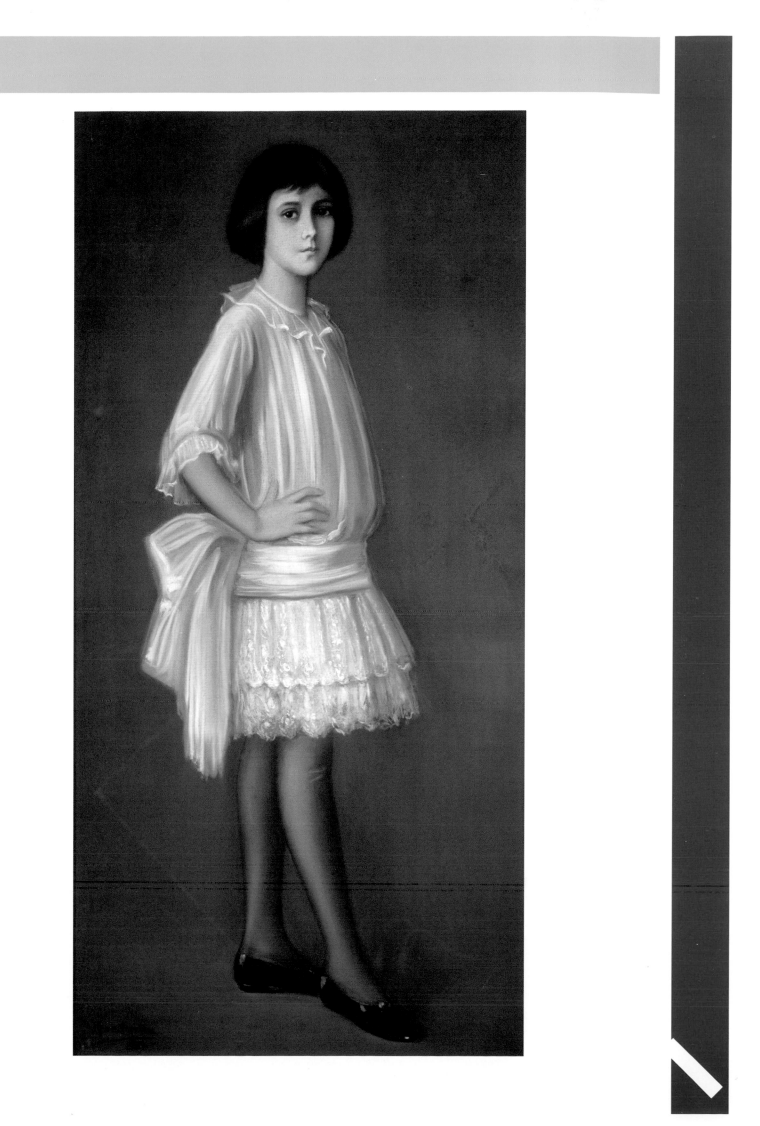

On Mondays,

Mondays in the summer,

I hug my cat, Hummer.

He's like a brother.

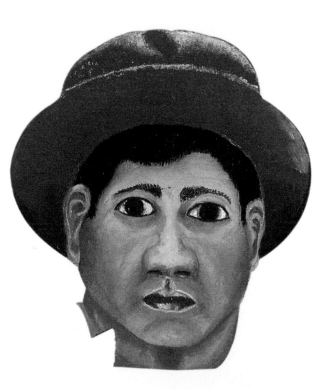

Boy with Cat
Fernando Castillo

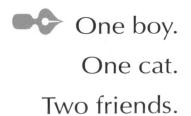 One boy.

One cat.

Two friends.

8

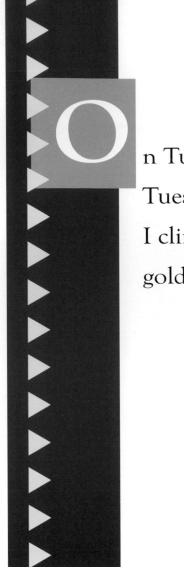

On Tuesdays,

Tuesdays in the fall,

I climb to the rooftop to see the moon,

golden, silvery, round as a ball.

Beds Made for Dreaming
Carmen Lomas Garza

One mother.

Two daughters.

Three people.

On Wednesdays,
Wednesdays in the winter,
my mother sews, my sister read,
and I am the writer.

Day's End
Diego Rivera

One mother.
Two girls.
Three children.
Four people in a family.

O n Thursdays,
Thursdays in the spring,
my parents and uncles talk,
about family, about caring.

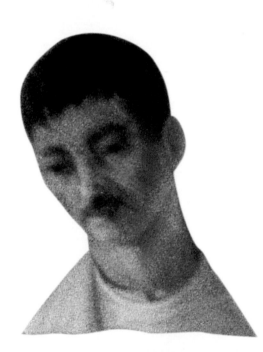

Andean Family
Héctor Poleo

 One girl.
Two young women.
Three men.
Four grown-ups.
Five people.

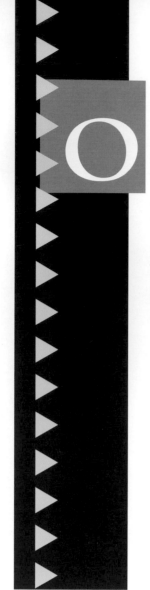

On Fridays,

Fridays in the summer,

everyone is up and working,

in the cool of the early morning.

Country Landscape
Roberto Benítez

 One pond.

Two oxen.

Three herons in the water.

Four men with sickles.

Five houses.

Six cactus plants.

On Saturdays,
Saturdays in the fall,
my cousins come to visit,
and we play ball!

My Family Before I Was Born
Luis Jaso

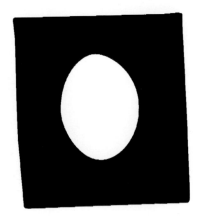

 One boy dressed in white.
Two women.
Three children.
Four grown-ups.
Five people dressed in black.
Six people without mustaches.
Seven people in a family.

O
n Sundays,

Sundays in the winter,

you do not hear a peep.

Everyone's in bed, asleep.

Central Railway of Brazil
Tarsila do Amaral

One church.

Two telephone poles.

Three palm trees.

Four wheels.

Five flags.

Six iron posts.

Seven blue windows.

Eight circles.

Monday or Tuesday,
Wednesday or Thursday,
Friday or Saturday or Sunday,
every day is a great day!
How about a party?
Hip, hip, hooray!

Dance in Tehuantepec
Diego Rivera

One man dressed in yellow.
Two hats.
Four people dancing.
Five women sitting.
Six ribbons on the posts.
Seven women in all.
Eight dancing feet.
Nine people at the dance.

In the summer or the fall,
In the winter or the spring,
the park fills with happy chattering.
Listen! Can you hear the laughter ring?

The Fair, Lupe, and Pancho
Ezequiel Negrete

One umbrella.
Two women standing.
Three colors on the umbrella.
Four street lamps.
Five balconies.
Six feet with sandals.
Seven windows.
Ten people around the umbrella.

DIEGO VELÁZQUEZ

Velázquez is one of the greatest painters of all time. Las Meninas is one of his most famous painings. He was the official painter during the reign of Philip IV of Spain and painted the royal family many times.

Las Meninas

The girl who appears surrounded by her maids, called *meninas,* was the daughter of Philip IV of Spain. If you look closely, you can see Velázquez in his painting. He is standing at his easel. On the back wall, there is a mirror and you can see the reflections of the king and queen. They must be visiting the painter's studio to observe as he paints their daughter. You will see that the king and queen are watching from our same vantage point.

ALFREDO RAMOS

Ramos was born in Mexico and received many awards for his innovative style. He founded the Open Air School of Art. He loved to paint portraits of girls and boys.

Dolores Asúnsolo at Age Eleven

When a painter paints a person who poses for him, the painting is called a *portrait*. "Portrait" is used in photography also. A portrait can be done in any style using any kind of material. Ramos used pastels in this painting. It is a *realistic portrait* because it reproduces reality much the way a photograph does.

FERNANDO CASTILLO

Castillo was born to a poor family in Mexico. His dream was to become a painter. Thanks to his dream and hard work, he became an important figure in Mexican art.

Boy with Cat

In this painting, a Mexican boy hugs his cat. The painter shows the love between them. The painting does not look like a photograph. Castillo wanted to paint them as they were, but he also expressed the feelings transmitted by the subjects, the boy and cat.

CARMEN LOMAS GARZA

This famous painter was born in Kingsville, Texas, to a Mexican family. Her love for painting was encouraged by her mother. Garza's paintings reflect life in the Mexican-American community. She captured her childhood experiences in charming detail.

Beds Made for Dreaming

The girls in this painting look at the sky and talk about their dreams. The artist painted scenes of everyday life exactly as she remembered it. This is called genre painting. Garza uses oils on canvas with the addition of traditional Mexican paper cut-outs.

⌐⌐ DIEGO RIVERA

Rivera was born in Guanajuato, Mexico, in 1886 and began painting as a child. As an adult he traveled to Spain, France, England, and Italy to see the great European classical paintings. Rivera returned to Mexico with the desire to paint the history and people of Mexico. Although he also painted on canvas, his favorite medium was the mural. Murals are large paintings on walls. Rivera died in 1957.

Day's End

⌐⌐ Everyday life was a favorite theme in Diego Rivera's paintings. Although he was influenced by cubism in the earlier part of his career, he later abandoned this style for a unique style of his own. This style is called *expressionism* and he used it for the rest of his life. *Day's End* is an expressionistic genre painting.

⌐⌐ HÉCTOR POLEO

Héctor Poleo (1918-1989) was born in Venezuela, where he studied at the School of Fine Arts. Although landscapes were the preferred paintings during his time, Hector went to Mexico to study with the great muralists, Orozco, Rivera, and Siqueiros. Upon his return to Venezuela, he put the human figure at the center of his work. His work was in a style of well-delineated, almost sculptural social realism.

Andean Family

⌐⌐ This painting shows us the beauty and significance of everday life. Poleo painted an Andean family, people who work the land, standing tall and proud.

ROBERTO BENÍTEZ

Naïf or primitive painters in Mexico have in common not only their style, but also their inspiration. Life in the fields and everyday life are constant themes in their paintings. Roberto Benítez is a painter from Oaxaca, Mexico.

Country Landscape

The fields offer both beauty and natural resources. These families work their fields as a team. When crops need to be harvested, all hands are needed. The artist has used oils on wood for this painting.

LUIS JASO

Luis Jaso was born in Mexico. His formal education in art was very limited, but he felt compelled to paint his surroundings from an early age. His favorite subjects were the members of his own family. He painted them constantly.

My Family Before I Was Born

Luis Jaso painted using live models. He also painted from photographs. This painting was probably based on a picture from the family album. It is done in a primitive style.

❧ TARSILA DO AMARAL

Tarsila do Amaral (1886-1973) was born in Brazil. She traveled to Europe at a young age to study modernist paintings. At first she painted geometric figures to create what is called a figurative scene. Later, after years of studying the human figure and the social reality in her country, she incorporated a modernist style in her work.

Central Railway of Brazil

❧ Tarsila do Amaral created a landscape with geometric figures in this painting. She used circles, squares, and triangles. Even though there are no people in the painting, the viewer feels the atmosphere of a bustling city, now at rest.

❧ DIEGO RIVERA

Diego Rivera has been recognized internationally as one of Mexico's greatest painters. His large mural paintings in public buildings tell the history of Mexico. Frequently we can see political figures from all over the world in his paintings. Sometimes his paintings were damaged or destroyed by people with different political views.

Dance in Tehuantepec

❧ Diego Rivera wanted to show the real life of his people. That is why many of his paintings reflect family and genre scenes, such as in the case of *Dance in Tehuantepec*.

☙ EZEQUIEL NEGRETE

Negrete (1902-1960) was born in Mexico City, where he studied at the San Carlos Academy. He was a student in the Open Air School of Art. These schools, popular at the turn of the century, devoted special attention to the social atmosphere of a scene and the reality of the subjects portrayed.

The Fair, Lupe, and Pancho

☙ People at home and in the streets, typical scenes of everyday life, were the preferred subjects of Negrete's paintings. In this painting, women and children try their luck at a spinning umbrella in hopes of winning some candy or a small cake.

ACKNOWLEDGEMENTS

Cover; page 5 / Diego Velázquez, *Las Meninas*.
Copyright © Museo del Prado / Madrid / All rights
reserved. Reproduction authorized by Museo del Prado.

Page 7 / Alfredo Ramos, *Dolores Asúnsolo at Age Eleven*.
Copyright © Consejo Nacional para la Cultura y las Artes
/ Instituto Nacional de Bellas Artes y Literatura / Museo
Nacional de Arte / Mexico.

Page 9 / Fernando Castillo, *Boy with Cat*. Copyright ©
Centro Popular de Pintura de San Antonio Abad / Gabriel
Fernández Ledesma Collection / Mexico. Extensive
research failed to locate the copyright holder of this work.

Page 11 / Carmen Lomas Garza, *Beds Made for
Dreaming*. Copyright ©1989 Carmen Lomas Garza.
Photo: Judy Reed. Reproduction authorized by Carmen
Lomas Garza.

Page 13 / Diego Rivera, *Day's End* (detail), 1926.
Copyright © 2000 Reproduction authorized by the
Instituto Nacional de Bellas Artes y Literatura and Banco
de México, Fiduciario en el Fideicomiso relativo a los
Museos Diego Rivera y Frida Kahlo.

Page 15 / Héctor Poleo, *Andean Family,* 1944. Copyright
© Art Museum of the Americas of the Organization of
American States / Permanent Collection (Gift of IBM).
Reproduction authorized by the Art Museum of the
Americas.

Page 17 / Roberto Benítez, *Country Landscape*. From the
collection of Alma Flor Ada and F. Isabel Campoy.

Page 19 / Luis Jaso, *My Family Before I Was Born,* 1963.
Copyright © Luis Jaso. Extensive research failed to locate
the copyright holder of this work.

Page 21 / Tarsila do Amaral, *Central Railway of
Brazil,* 1924. Copyright © Collection: Museu de Arte
Contemporânea da Universidade de São Paulo / Brazil.
Photo: Romulo Fialdini. Reproduction authorized by the
Museu de Arte Contemporânea.

Page 23 / Diego Rivera, *Dance in Tehuantepec* (detail),
1935. Copyright © 2000 Reproduction authorized by the
Instituto Nacional de Bellas Artes y Literatura and Banco
de México, Fiduciario en el Fideicomiso relativo a los
Museos Diego Rivera y Frida Kahlo.

Page 25 / Ezequiel Negrete, *The Fair, Lupe, and Pancho,*
1954. From the collection of the Instituto Nacional de
Bellas Artes y Literatura / Mexico.